Savvy

Calm

Girl

Yoga for STRESS RELIEF

by Rebecca Rissman

CAPSTONE PRESS
a capstone imprint

Savvy Books are published by Capstone Press.
1710 Roe Crest Drive, North Mankato, Minnesota 56003
www.capstonepub.com

Library of Congress Cataloging-in-Publication Data

Cataloging-in-Publication Data in on file with the Library of Congress.

ISBN 978-1-4914-2121-5 (library binding)
ISBN 978-1-4914-2362-2 (eBook PDF)

Editorial Credits
Mandy Robbins, editor; Heidi Thompson, designer; Sarah Schuette, prop preparation; Marcy Morin, scheduler; Charmaine Whitman, production specialist

Photo Credits
Capstone Studio: TJ Thoraldson Digital Photography, all photos except; Shutterstock: Dean Drobot, 61, Kandelaki, 7, Lana K, 58-59, Maridav, 10. Design Elements: Shutterstock: A-R-T, redstone, vectorkat

Printed in Canada.
092014   008478FRS15

TABLE OF
Contents

Feeling
Stressed?

Stop biting your nails and put down that stress ball. There's a better way to deal with anxiety that won't wreck your manicure. Why not give yoga a try? It's the ultimate workout for any super-stressed girl.

Yoga is a great activity to turn to when you feel overwhelmed. It combines controlled breathing, physical poses, and meditation to help you calm down and save your cuticles. After even a short yoga practice, you'll be feeling more serene.

Most types of yoga will help you chill out, but some are specifically geared toward stress relief. If you want to move through different relaxing poses slowly, enjoying each one for several minutes, try Yin Yoga. It has a slow pace and focuses on alignment. If you want something a bit more active, try Restorative Yoga.

Some yoga poses are especially helpful when you need to calm down. Poses that allow you to sit or lie down are great for stress relief. So are gentle twists. Try to add these into your yoga practice the next time you can't stop your thoughts from racing.

An Ancient
CURE FOR STRESS

Are you busy juggling family, school, friends, and time for yourself? Or maybe you're balancing sports, the debate team, and other extra-curricular activities. Adding an activity such as yoga to your life might seem like the last thing you need, but give it a try. Doing yoga is an excellent way to reduce your stress levels. In fact, yoga has been helping people improve their lives for thousands of years.

People started practicing yoga in Ancient India as a way to grow spiritually. Some of yoga's roots come from the Eastern religions Hinduism, Buddhism, and Jainism. Many of the names of yoga poses are in Sanskrit, an ancient Indian language. However, modern American yoga is quite different from its ancient roots. Most Americans who practice yoga don't do it for religious reasons. Instead, they do it to get fit, increase their energy, and feel less stressed.

Most people think that yoga is about 5,000 years old, but it could be even older. A 5,000-year-old stone carving found in the Indus Valley (between modern northwestern India and Pakistan) shows a figure sitting in a yoga position.

Make Your Yoga
Sessions
Peaceful

Quick—you rush out of your tutoring session, grab your gym bag, and sprint to your mom's car. You have 30 minutes to squeeze in a quick yoga practice in your bedroom before dinner.

If this sounds like you, you're probably going to have a hard time relaxing when you finally roll out your yoga mat. And who wouldn't? You can't rush, rush, rush, and then expect to suddenly chill out.

In order to make your yoga practice as relaxing as possible, follow these tips:

- Slow down! You might not have time for an hour-long yoga practice, but any amount will be helpful. Focus on being calm and steady. Try to be relaxed as you set up your mat, props, and water for your practice.

- Turn off your cell phone. You won't be as relaxed if you're worried it will ring or if you're thinking about who might be texting you.

- Ask your family to give you privacy during your yoga practice. Knowing that nobody will barge in on you will help you relax.

- Play calm, quiet music that soothes you.

You know what isn't relaxing? Getting injured. Never do any yoga poses that cause you to feel pain. If something doesn't feel right, stop doing it immediately.

GET
WARMED Up

Some people react to stress by tightening or tensing some of their muscles. When you do a variety of yoga poses, you will be able to release any muscle tension you might have.

Warming up your muscles before you stretch them will help you avoid becoming injured. This is why it's important to do strength-building yoga poses at the beginning of your practice. Lunges, squats, and poses that work your core are all great ways to get warm.

In addition to helping you relax tight muscles, the physical practice of yoga also helps you to release nervous energy. Do you ever feel like your heart is racing, and you can't calm down? If so, yoga can be a great way to blow off some steam.

When you're practicing yoga, make sure to do standing poses, seated poses, twists, and forward folds. If any areas of your body feel particularly tight, spend extra time on poses that work and stretch those areas. After you've worked up a good sweat and relaxed some of your muscles, you'll have an easier time relaxing and de-stressing.

Ever notice that you've got a stiff neck or painful lower back during a stressful time in your life? Yoga could be just what the doctor ordered.

11

LOCUST POSE

Sanskrit Name: *Salabhasana*

Pronounced: shah-lah-BAHS-ah-nah

Do you hold tension in your back when you get stressed? If so, you might feel some slight back pain or discomfort when you're doing something that makes you anxious. Alternating Locust Pose with belly rests is a great way to work and relax the muscles in your back, neck, and legs.

step 1 Lie on your belly with your arms down along your sides.

step 2 Bring your forehead down onto the mat. Have your hands resting on the mat with your palms facing up and your thumbs touching your outer thighs. Point your toes, and allow the tops of your feet to rest on the mat.

Point your toes.

step 3   Lift your head, chest, and legs away from the floor. Keep your legs very straight.

step 4   Pull your shoulders away from your ears as you lift your hands up off the mat. Point your fingers toward your lifted heels to lengthen the arms.

step 5   Look slightly upward. Hold for a few breaths.

step 6   Slowly lower all the way down onto your mat. Turn your head to rest your right ear down onto the mat. Take a few restful breaths.

step 7   Repeat a few times, resting the opposite ear down onto the mat each time.

➡ If looking upward feels painful or uncomfortable, modify this pose by looking straight ahead or down at your mat.

Pull your shoulders away from your ears.

Look slightly upward.

WINDSHIELD WIPER POSE

Sometimes, holding perfectly still makes it hard to relax. You might find your thoughts wandering or feel tension creeping into your shoulders. If that's the case, try Windshield Wiper Pose. This is a gentle, rocking movement you can do to stretch your hips, abdomen, and legs.

 step 1 Lie on your back with your legs outstretched. Extend your arms out to your sides in a T shape.

 step 2 Bend your knees up. Place your feet on the mat just outside of your hips and a few inches in front of your bottom.

Step 2

Face your palms upward.

14

step 3   As you exhale, allow both knees to fall over to the right. You will feel a deep stretch down your left side. Keep your back flat on the mat and your arms relaxed.

step 4   As you inhale, use the muscles of your core to bring your knees back to the center.

step 5   Exhale and allow both knees to fall over to the left. This time, you will feel a deep stretch down your right side.

step 6   Continue in this gentle sequence. Try to link each movement to your breath. If it helps you to relax, try closing your eyes.

If this stretch feels intense, don't worry about bringing your foot close to your bottom. Instead, keep your arm straight.

HALF-FROG POSE

Sanskrit Name: *Ardha Bhekasana*

Pronounced: ARE-duh bay-KAHS-ah-nah

Half-Frog Pose stretches the muscles in your legs, back, and abdomen. Hold this pose while focusing on your breath and alignment. Try your best to stay focused in Half-Frog Pose. If you get distracted, close your eyes.

step 1 Lie on your belly on your mat.

step 2 Bring your legs together, and point your toes.

Point your elbow up.

Press into your forearm to lift your chest and shoulders up.

step 3   Bring your right elbow under your right shoulder to press up into a small backbend. Then keep your elbow where it is as you bring your right hand under your left shoulder with your palm facing down. This will make your right forearm parallel to the top of your mat.

step 4   Bend your left knee. Reach back with your left hand to grasp the inner edge of your left foot. Pull your foot toward the left side of your bottom. If you are able to, turn your left hand so that your fingers point forward and your palm presses into the top of your left foot with your elbow pointing up.

step 5   Press into your right forearm to lift your chest and shoulders farther away from the mat. Square your shoulders by pressing your left shoulder forward and pulling your right shoulder back. Drop your shoulders away from your ears.

step 6   Slowly let go of the left foot. Return to your belly to rest.

step 7   Repeat on the other side.

If this stretch feels intense, don't worry about bringing your foot close to your bottom. Instead, keep your arm straight.

WARRIOR 2

Sanskrit Name: *Virabhadrasana*

Pronounced: vee-rah-bah-DRAS-ah-nah

Warrior 2 Pose works your legs, arms, and back. In many yoga classes, teachers challenge students to hold this pose for several breaths at a time. When you are holding Warrior 2 Pose, it's easy to allow your mind to wander to worries or stresses in your life. Resist this by focusing on your alignment and breathing.

Keep your arms parallel to the ground.

step 1 From a standing position, take a big step forward with your left leg. Point your left toes straight ahead.

step 2 Bend the left knee deeply while you keep your right leg as straight as you can. Turn your right heel down so that your whole foot is touching the mat.

step 3 Turn your hips to face the right side of your mat.

step 4 Extend your arms out to your sides, with your palms facing down. Pull your shoulder blades together and down your back to make space between your shoulders and your ears.

step 5 Look out over your left thumb.

Keep your back leg as straight as you can.

step 6 Hold this for several breaths. Keep the deep bend in your left knee and focus on keeping your right leg very straight and strong.

step 7 Repeat on the other side.

Your front knee should hover right above your front ankle in this pose.

REVERSE WARRIOR

Reverse Warrior is a pose that often follows Warrior 2 Pose. It has all the benefits of Warrior 2, but with an additional deep side stretch that will really help release tension. Try flowing, or moving gracefully, between Warrior 2 and Reverse Warrior. Exhale into Warrior 2 Pose, and inhale into Reverse Warrior. Make each movement last as long as your breath. You can do this as many times as you like.

Face your palm to the floor.

Look up.

step 1 Start in Warrior 2 Pose with your left foot forward.

step 2 Flip your left palm in to face your body.

step 3 Bring your right hand down to the outside of your right thigh and reach your left hand straight up.

step 4 Slowly start to slide your right hand farther down your right leg. Reach your left arm toward the back of your mat to deeply stretch your left side.

step 5 Look up.

step 6 Return to Warrior 2 Pose.

step 7 Flow between these two poses several times.

step 8 Repeat on the opposite side.

If the back bend in Reverse Warrior feels too intense, extend your left arm straight up.

21

SEATED WIDE-ANGLE FORWARD FOLD

Sanskrit Name: *Upavistha Konasana*

Pronounced: OOH-pah-veesh-tah cone-AHS-ah-nah

Seated Wide-Angle Forward Fold stretches your legs, back, pelvis, and hips. It's important to keep your mind focused on your alignment. If you relax too much in this pose, you could overstretch your muscles and potentially become injured. Focusing on your alignment will also clear your mind of any other thoughts.

step 1 Sit on your mat with your legs outstretched.

step 2 Separate your legs as wide as you can while keeping your hips angled slightly forward. To do this, arch your back and point your tailbone slightly out behind you.

step 3 Flex your feet, and point your toes and kneecaps straight up.

step 4 Bring your fingertips just in front of your hips on the mat. Straighten your back by lifting the crown of your head straight up.

step 5 Keep your feet flexed and your hips still. Very slowly, walk your fingertips forward until you feel a stretch in your pelvis, legs, and back. You might not walk your fingers very far forward—don't worry. Just find a position that feels challenging for you.

step 6 Hold for a few breaths.

step 7 Slowly walk your hands back in toward your body to come out of this pose.

Did separating your legs make it hard for you to sit upright? Did you feel like you needed to tuck your tailbone under you to keep this stretch? If so, sit on a block or a folded yoga blanket. This will make it easier to keep your hips even.

Point your kneecaps straight up.

Flex your feet.

23

SEATED WIDE-ANGLE FORWARD FOLD VARIATIONS

Once you've learned the basics of Seated Wide-Angle Forward Fold, you can have fun playing with different variations of it. The twisted version is a nice way to stretch the spine and lower back. For an invigorating abdominal stretch try the side-opening version.

TWISTED SEATED WIDE-ANGLE FORWARD FOLD

step 1 Start in Seated Wide-Angle Forward Fold.

step 2 Sit up very tall by lifting the crown of your head up. Pull your belly button in toward your spine.

step 3 Bring your hands to either side of your right thigh. Point your belly button toward your right kneecap.

step 4 Keep your back as straight as you can, and keep both feet flexed with your toes pointing up. Walk your hands toward your right foot. Stop when you feel challenged.

Step 2

step 5 Hold for a few breaths.

step 6 Walk your hands back in toward your hips to rest.

step 7 Repeat on the other side.

24

SIDE OPENING SEATED WIDE-ANGLE FORWARD FOLD

Step 2

step 1 Start in Seated Wide-Angle Forward Fold.

step 2 Sit up very tall by lifting the crown of your head up. Pull your belly button in toward your spine.

step 3 Lift your right hand up.

step 4 Bring your left hand to the mat in front of you.

step 5 Turn your chest open to the right. Begin to stretch the right side of your body by reaching your right hand toward the left.

step 6 Hold for a few breaths.

step 7 Repeat on the other side.

TWISTED HEAD-TO-KNEE POSE

Sanskrit Name: *Parivrtta Janu Sirsasana*

Pronounced: pahr-VREE-tah JAH-new seer-SAHS-ah-nah

Are you ready for more of a challenge? Twisted Head-to-Knee Pose takes the stretch you got in the previous pose and adds a bind and hip stretch. Try this pose after you've worked on Side Opening Seated Wide-Angle Forward Fold to get the maximum benefits.

step 1 Start in a seated position with your legs outstretched.

step 2 Bring your left heel into the inside of your left thigh. Allow your left knee to fall out to the left.

step 3   Open your right leg out to the right as far as you can. Keep your right leg straight, and turn your right toes and kneecap up.

step 4   Bring your right forearm down onto the mat on the inside of your right shin, with your palm facing up.

step 5   Lift your left arm straight up.

step 6   Twist your chest open to the left.

step 7   Start to reach your left arm up and over toward your right foot. If you can, try to grasp your right big toe with your left hand. Grasp the inner edge of your right foot with your right hand as well. Holding the right foot with one or both hands is a bind.

step 8   Hold for a few breaths.

step 9   Repeat on the other side.

If you can't reach your left hand to your right foot, don't worry. Just think about turning your chest open and stretching your left side.

LEGS UP THE WALL POSE

Sanskrit Name: *Viparita Karani*

Pronounced: vee-pah-REE-tah car-AHN-ee

Inversions are yoga poses that bring the head below the heart. Most of the time, we think of poses like handstands and headstands as inversions. However, Legs Up the Wall Pose is a relaxing inversion that can help you de-stress.

step 1 Set a yoga bolster on your yoga mat about 6 inches (15 centimeters) away from a wall that doesn't have any shelves, pictures, or windows that you might bump. If you don't have a bolster, you could try using a pillow or a rolled-up blanket or sweatshirt.

step 2 Carefully lay your lower back onto the bolster with your legs up the wall. This will take a little maneuvering. Scoot closer to the wall until your bottom is resting up against it. Your head and shoulders should rest comfortably on the mat.

step 3 Bring your feet together on the wall. Straighten your legs as much as you can.

step 4 Extend your arms out to the sides with your elbows bent and palms facing up.

step 5 Pull your shoulders down away from your ears. Gently rock your head from side to side to release any tension from your neck.

You might need to shift the bolster closer to the wall, or you might want to have it a bit farther away. Take a few minutes to get comfortable.

step 6 Close your eyes and be as still as you can.

step 7 Hold this position for several breaths.

step 8 Roll to one side to come out of this pose. Rest on your side for a few breaths.

VARIATIONS ON LEGS UP THE WALL POSE

If you love the Legs Up the Wall Pose, you might want to try a few variations on it. You can do many different leg positions in this pose. Just remember to rest on your side when you finish. Spending an extended amount of time with your legs raised could make you dizzy.

BOUND ANGLE VARIATION

 step 1   Start in Legs Up the Wall Pose.

step 2   Bring the soles of your feet together, and allow your knees to fall to the sides.

step 3   Slide your feet down the wall toward your hips.

step 4   Using the muscles in your legs, press your knees toward the wall.

step 5   Hold for several breaths.

step 6   Return to Legs Up the Wall Pose, then rest on your side.

Step 1

WIDE-LEGGED VARIATION OF LEGS UP THE WALL POSE

step 1 Start in Legs Up the Wall Pose.

step 2 Allow the legs to fall out to the sides until you feel a stretch in your pelvis.

step 3 Keep your feet flexed, and pull your kneecaps in toward your hips. Hold your legs where you feel the stretch, and breathe deeply.

step 4 Use your hands to help press your legs together to come back to Legs Up the Wall Pose. Then rest on your side.

Step 1

Flex your feet ——

31

HALF LORD OF THE FISHES POSE

Sanskrit Name: *Ardha Matsyendrasana*

Pronounced: ARE-duh mot-see-on-DRAHS-ah-nah

This twisting pose will definitely help you relieve stress.
Many people hold muscle tension in their necks and shoulders.
Half Lord of the Fishes Pose focuses on relaxing these tense areas.

step 1 Start in a seated position with your legs extended.

step 2 Bend your right knee up, and step your right foot just outside of your left knee.

step 3 Bend your left knee, and bring your left foot just outside of your right hip. This might take a bit of wiggling. Feel free to use your hands to get your foot in the right place.

step 4 Bring your right hand to the mat behind your hips. Straighten your right elbow, and sit up very tall.

step 5 Reach your left arm straight up. Make as much space as you can between your left ribs and your left hip.

step 6 Twist to the right, bringing your left elbow to the outside of your right knee. Turn your palm to face open to the right side of the mat.

step 7 Look over your right shoulder.

step 8 Hold for a few breaths and repeat on the other side.

If you aren't quite able to get your elbow to the outside of your knee, don't worry. A simple way to modify this pose is to hold the knee with your hand instead.

Keep your back straight.

MARICHI'S POSE

Sanskrit Name: *Marichyasana 3*

Pronounced: mar-ee-chee-AHS-ah-nah

Marichi's Pose looks a bit like Half Lord of the Fishes, but it stretches different areas. Remember to breathe deeply while doing Marichi's Pose. The deep twist and abdominal work, combined with slow and relaxed breathing, will have you feeling calm in no time.

Keep your back straight.

step 1   Start in a seated position with your legs extended.

step 2   Bend your right knee straight up, and pull your right heel as close into your right hip as you can.

step 3   Keep your left leg very straight. Flex your left foot so that your toes and kneecap point up.

step 4   Bring your right hand behind your hips. Straighten your right elbow.

step 5   Straighten your back as much as you can to sit up very tall. You will need to use your core muscles to do this. Pull your belly button in toward your spine, and reach up through the crown of your head.

step 6   Reach your left hand straight up into the air. Make as much space as you can between your left ribs and your left hip.

step 7   Twist to the right, bringing your left elbow to the outside of your right knee. Turn your palm to face open to the right side of the mat.

step 8   Look over your right shoulder.

step 9   Hold for several breaths.

step 10   Repeat on the other side.

One of the hardest parts of this pose is keeping your back upright. Be patient and keep working on it.

Flex your feet.

Feel free to modify this pose in the same way you did for Half Lord of the Fishes Pose. If the twist is too intense for you, simply hold your knee with your hand instead of resting your elbow on the outside of your knee.

WALL DOG POSE

Many people carry tension in their neck, shoulders, and upper back. This shoulder-opening pose encourages you to release tension in those areas. It is also a good stretch for the muscles in your legs. Try this pose when you need to take a break from your homework.

step 1 Stand facing a wall with no windows or objects hanging from it.

step 2 Place your palms on the wall shoulder-distance apart at the height of your elbows.

step 3 Walk your feet about 3 feet (1 meter) back away from the wall. Bend at the hips to bring your upper body horizontal. Keep your hips over your feet.

step 4 Press your hands into the wall until you feel a deep stretch in your shoulders.

step 5 Pull your belly button in toward your spine.

step 6 Keep your legs as straight as you can. Press into all parts of your feet.

Keep your back parallel to the ground.

Try not to let your upper body sag down toward the floor. Keep firm pressure in your hands to keep your upper body parallel to the floor.

CHILD'S POSE

Sanskrit Name: *Balasana*

Pronounced: bah-LAHS-ah-nah

Need a quick way to chill out? Do a few yoga poses to work and stretch your body, and then drop into Child's Pose for a few minutes. Before you know it, you'll feel less anxious and stressed. You might even feel a little sleepy.

step 1 Start on your hands and knees.

step 2 Bring your knees a bit farther apart and make your big toes touch.

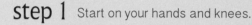

Get comfortable. Experiment with having your knees closer together or farther apart until you feel as though you could stay in this pose comfortably. If your neck feels stiff, try rocking your head gently from side to side before becoming still with your forehead on the mat.

step 3 Sit your bottom down onto your heels and bring your forehead down to the mat.

step 4 Stretch out your arms in front of you. Lay your palms flat on the mat.

step 5 Press into your palms to straighten your elbows, and press your bottom into your heels.

step 6 Relax your upper body and allow your forearms to rest on the mat.

step 7 Hold for several breaths.

Don't be afraid to modify this pose. If your shoulders are especially tight try resting your arms down along your sides. This modification will help lengthen and relax the muscles in your neck and shoulders.

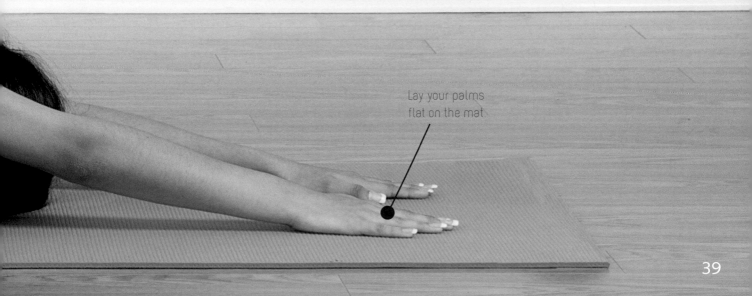

Lay your palms flat on the mat.

RECLINED HERO'S POSE

Sanskrit Name: *Supta Virasana*

Pronounced: SOUP-ta veer-AHS-ah-nah

Reclined Hero's Pose stretches the muscles in your feet, hips and thighs while allowing you to close your eyes and rest on your back. Try your best to relax the muscles in your jaw, shoulders, and lower back while in this pose.

step 1 From your hands and knees, separate your feet so that they are slightly wider than your hips. Press the tops of your feet down into the mat.

step 2 Walk your hands back toward the outsides of your hips as you slowly sit between your heels.

step 3 Slowly, walk your hands behind you to begin to tilt your upper body back. With control, lower all the way onto your back. Do not allow your knees to lift away from the mat.

step 4 Press your tailbone forward.

step 5 Allow your hands to rest comfortably down at your sides.

step 6 Close your eyes and breathe deeply.

Remember—don't do any pose that causes you pain. If the stretch described here feels too intense, stop at Step 2.

RECLINED BIG TOE POSE

Sanskrit Name: *Supta Padangusthasana*

Pronounced: SOUP-tah pah-dan-goose-TAHS-ah-nah

Are you ready for a rest? Reclined Big Toe Pose can be done standing or lying down. But don't be fooled! The reclined version is just as difficult—because you have to stay mentally balanced. Don't let your mind wander while doing this pose. Just think about your breath and alignment.

step 1 Lie on your back with your legs outstretched.

step 2 Loop your yoga strap around your right foot, and extend your right leg up. Hold the strap with your right hand. Straighten your right leg as much as you can.

step 3 Keep your left leg straight. Point your left toes and kneecap up. Press your left hip and heel into the mat.

step 4 Press your left hand down into the mat outside your left hip. Use your right hand to pull your right leg close to you. At the same time, press your right heel away from you. This will create muscular tension in the right leg.

Flex your feet.

Are you super flexible? If so, drop the strap and hold onto your big toe with your thumb, index, and middle fingers.

step 5 Hold this for a few breaths.

step 6 Repeat on the other side.

VARIATIONS ON RECLINED BIG TOE POSE

Try these relaxing variations on Reclined Big Toe Pose. They stretch different parts of your hips, back, and legs. They are also a great way to wind down at the end of a challenging yoga workout. Just remember to keep your thoughts focused on the sound of your breath. Worrying about your homework won't help you de-stress.

HIP OPENING RECLINED BIG TOE POSE

step 1 Start in Reclined Big Toe Pose with your left leg extended into the air. Loop a yoga strap around your left foot, and hold it with your left hand. Be sure to keep both shoulders on the mat.

step 2 Press your right hand firmly down onto your right hip. Do not let your right hip lift away from the mat. Press all parts of your right leg down into the mat. Keep your right foot flexed, and point your right toes and kneecap straight up.

Step 1

step 3 Slowly start to pull your left leg open to the left. You will feel this stretch in the left side of your groin. Keep your left leg as straight as possible, and flex your left foot.

step 4 When you feel this stretch becoming intense, stop and hold the pose. Take a few deep breaths.

step 5 Repeat on the other side.

CROSS-BODY RECLINED BIG TOE POSE

step 1 Start in Reclined Big Toe Pose with your left leg extended into the air. Loop a yoga strap around your left foot and hold it with your left hand. Press both shoulder blades into the mat.

step 2 Push your left hip into the mat. This will help lengthen the left side of your body.

step 3 Very slowly use your left hand to pull your left leg over to the right. Keep your left hip down on the mat. Your leg won't go very far over to the right, but you'll feel this stretch right away.

step 4 Repeat on the other side.

Step 1

RECLINED TWIST

Sanskrit Name: *Supta Matsyendrasana*

Pronounced: SOUP-tah mot-see-en-DRAHS-ah-nah

A lot of people carry tension in their neck and back. Try to relax while you lie down and work out that tension. With Reclined Twist you'll enjoy the deep stretch in your neck, back, and as an added bonus, your legs.

step 1 Lie on your back with your legs outstretched.

step 2 Keep your left leg outstretched on your mat. Pull your right knee into your chest and give it a hug with both arms. Squeeze your knee in tightly.

step 3 Extend your right arm out onto the mat, palm facing down.

step 4 Use your left hand to pull your right knee to the left. If it's possible, bring the inside of your right knee to the mat outside your left hip.

step 5 Extend your left hand out onto the mat, palm facing down.

step 6 Turn your head to the right. Close your eyes and hold this for a few breaths.

step 7 Repeat on the other side.

Stack your hips.

RECLINED BOUND ANGLE POSE

Sanskrit Name: *Supta Baddha Konasana*

Pronounced: SOUP-tah BAHD-ah cone-AHS-ah-nah

Do you need to take a load off? Reclined Bound Angle Pose is a great way to chill out. Enjoy this calming, restorative pose for as long as you like. You can hold it for a few breaths or even while you take a short nap. Your hips, lower back, neck, and shoulders will thank you for it.

step 1 Start out sitting. Bring the soles of your feet together, and let your knees fall to the sides.

step 2 Slide your feet closer to your body until you begin to feel a stretch in your hips. Don't worry about how close you can bring your heels into your body. This will be a different distance for everyone.

step 3 Slowly, lower your back down onto the floor.

step 4 Press your elbows firmly into the mat to briefly lift your upper body about an inch off the mat. With your back lifted, pull your shoulder blades closer together. Then relax onto your mat again. Your back should feel supported.

step 5 Extend your arms down at your sides. Have your palms face up.

step 6 Hold for several breaths.

If this pose feels too intense prop up your knees with bolsters or pillows. Doing this will reduce the intensity of the stretch.

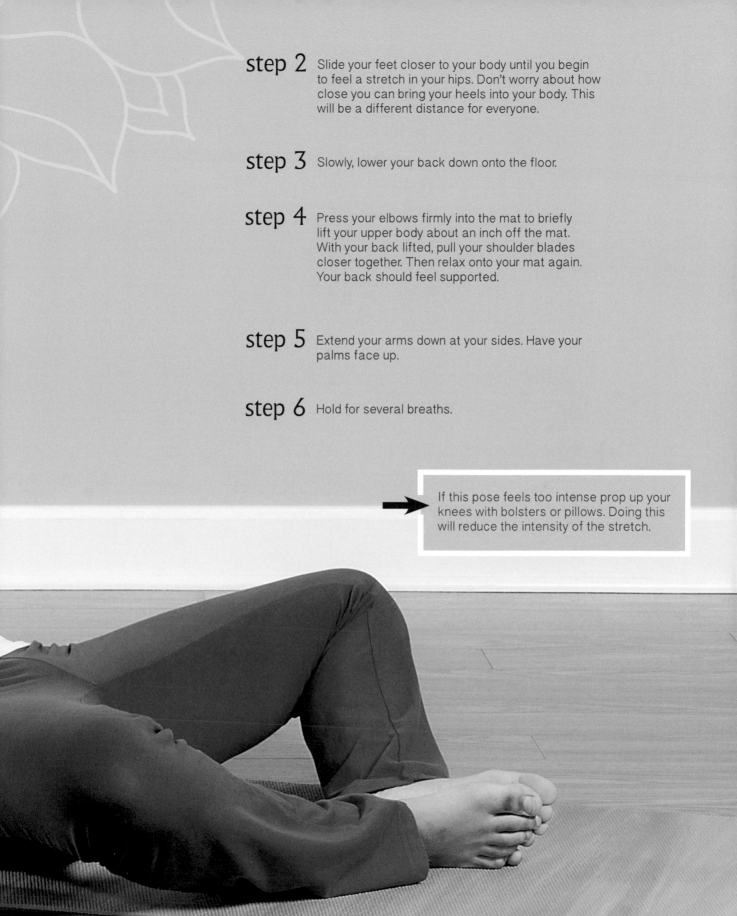

HAPPY BABY POSE

Sanskrit Name: *Ananda Balasana*

Pronounced: on-ON-duh ball-AHS-ah-nah

Have you ever seen a baby happily playing with her feet?
Channel your inner child in this carefree pose. Let yourself
move and stretch in whatever ways feel good to you.

step 1 Lie on your back on your yoga mat.

step 2 Pull both of your knees into your chest. Hold the outsides of your knees with both hands and squeeze them tightly into your chest.

step 3 Keeping your knees close in to your body, extend your feet up.

step 4 Grasp the outer edges of your feet with your hands.

step 5 Pull your feet straight down toward the outer edges of your mat. Your knees will be splayed.

step 6 Get creative. Rock from side to side, or straighten one or both legs at a time. Feel free to explore this pose until you find a variation that feels good on your hips, legs, and back.

step 7 Stay in this pose for several breaths. Don't worry about holding still. If movement feels good in this pose, move.

Let your knees fall out to the sides of your body.

51

RECLINED PIGEON POSE

Between school, studying at home, and the occasional TV session, you probably spend a lot of time sitting. All that chair time can make your hips stiff. Try this relaxing pose to release tension from your hips and lower back. Spend some time exploring how your body feels while you do this pose.

step 1 Lie down on your mat.

step 2 Bend your knees up and step your feet onto the mat just in front of your bottom.

Flex your feet.

step 3 Lift your left foot off the mat and cross it over your right knee. Try to rest the left ankle just outside the right knee. This will make this pose a bit more comfortable.

step 4 Flex your left foot so that the toes pull back toward the knee.

step 5 Lift your right foot off the mat, and pull your right knee in toward your chest.

step 6 Interlace your fingers on the back of the right thigh by bringing your left hand inside the leg and your right hand outside the leg.

step 7 Use the muscles in your left leg to press your left knee away from your chest. At the same time, use your arms to pull your right thigh closer to your chest.

step 8 Hold for a few breaths.

step 9 Repeat on the other side.

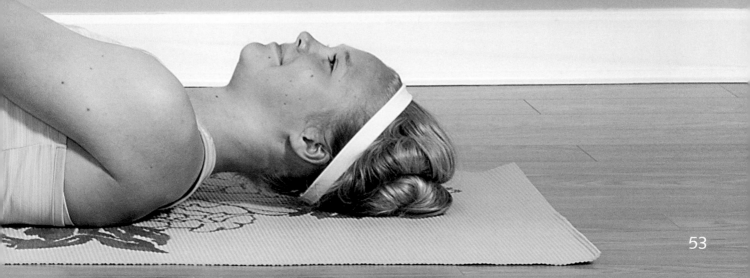

CORPSE POSE

Sanskrit Name: *Savasana*

Pronounced: sah-VAHS-ah-nah

You're brave. But are you brave enough to try something called Corpse Pose? Get comfortable. That's the most important rule for practicing Corpse Pose. You won't be able to fully relax if you're thinking about how your back is hurting, or if you need to take your hair out of your ponytail.

step 1 Get rid of anything that might distract you. If you're wearing glasses, take them off. If your hair is up in a tight or restrictive style, take it down.

step 2 Lie down onto your back.

step 3 Extend your legs out away from you. Separate your heels so that they are almost as wide as your mat.

Warm up. If you're in a room that is chilly, put on a long sleeve shirt over your yoga clothes. You might want to put on a pair of socks too.

Corpse Pose is often done at the end of a yoga practice. However, feel free to do it whenever you need a little rest or relaxation!

step 4 Bring your arms down to your sides, palms facing up.

step 5 Adjust. Roll from side to side to get rid of any tightness in your back. Turn your head from side to side to release tension in your neck.

step 6 Relax. Release any tension from the muscles in your face and jaw. Drop your tongue away from the roof of your mouth.

step 7 Breathe deeply. Close your eyes. Try to become as still as possible.

step 8 Hold for several minutes.

step 9 Slowly roll to one side. Rest on your side for a few breaths before sitting up.

CORPSE POSE
continued

Corpse Pose is one of yoga's most important poses. In fact, some might say that Corpse Pose is the only pose that really matters. The goal of Corpse Pose is to achieve a state of mental and physical stillness. This is difficult to do because it's always tempting to scratch an itch or allow your mind to wander. But don't be discouraged. Use the lessons you've learned in your yoga practice to keep your mind focused on your breath instead of any distractions or worries. It won't be easy, but be patient.

Corpse Pose is traditionally done at the very end of a yoga practice. The fatigue you feel at that point will make it easier for you to completely relax. Corpse Pose can last from a few minutes to half an hour or even more. Some yoga teachers might play music, chant, or sing during Corpse Pose. Others will keep the yoga room very quiet. Most people prefer to practice Corpse Pose in the dark. Allow your tired muscles to completely relax. Let your breath come naturally. Close your eyes. Do your best to ignore any ideas that pop up in your mind.

Experiencing tightness or pain in your lower back while in Corpse Pose? Place a bolster under your knees when you lie down.

Eye Pillow

Eye pillows are helpful props to have on hand during Corpse Pose. These small rectangles of fabric are usually filled with rice, seeds, or beans. Sometimes they are even filled with pleasant-smelling herbs. If you're having trouble relaxing in Corpse Pose, place an eye pillow over your eyes when you lie down in this final posture. The gentle pressure of the pillow over your eyes will help you relax.

Yoga for SLEEP

Stress during the daytime is bad enough. But losing sleep over it is the worst. Use the lessons you've learned from yoga to deal with your stress, even in the middle of the night.

Sleep Guru

Recent studies have shown that people who practice yoga sleep better than those who do not.

First, make sure your sleeping space is as relaxing as possible. Just as you set up a quiet space for your yoga practice, make sure your bedroom is as calm as possible. Your sleep environment is important. If it's loud, light, or distracting, you'll have trouble getting quality sleep. Try these tricks for making your room into a Zen zone:

- Make the room as dark as possible. Close the curtains, and turn off any nightlights, lamps, or electronics with lights.

- Keep your laptop and cell phone in another room.

- Turn off your music.

- Ask your family to respect your privacy at night.

When you lie down for bed at night, imagine you are going to practice Corpse Pose. Get as comfortable as you can. Make gentle movements to release any muscular tension you have. Then try to relax all of your muscles. Don't forget about the muscles in your face. Finally, try to think only about the sound of your breath. Before you know it, you'll be dreaming.

Relaxation
CHECKLIST

Feeling anxious about your test? Worried that you're being left out at school? Stressed about this Friday's big game? Follow these quick directions to help release some muscle tension:

- Unclench your jaw.

- Release the muscles in your shoulders.

- Relax the muscles in your lower back.

- Gently rock your head from side to side to release the muscles in your neck.

- Drop your tongue away from the roof of your mouth.

Use Yoga to Stay Relaxed at School

Life is stressful. A girl like you can't always drop everything and hit her yoga mat to work through the latest drama. So how can you chill out on the go? It's easy. Just summon your yoga brain wherever you are.

Yoga teaches us to move slowly and carefully through different poses, focusing on our alignment and breath. Try to think this way about everything you do in life. Take things step-by-step. Whenever you feel overwhelmed, slow down and focus on your breath.

Yoga is more than just physical exercise. It's a way to exercise your brain and learn to control your thoughts. The more you work on staying focused and calm during yoga, the easier it will be in other areas of your life. Learning to take life one step at a time is one of the greatest benefits of practicing yoga.

Deep Breathing

Seeing red? Crazy stressed? Stop what you're doing. Slowly inhale and count to six. Then exhale as you count to six. Keep doing this, extending your inhales and exhales to last for the entire six beats. Focusing on your breath and repeating the simple sequence of numbers will help you calm down.

Glossary

alignment (uh-LYNE-muhnt)—the correct positioning of the body in order to reduce the chance of injury

core (KOHR)—the muscles of your stomach, chest, back and pelvis

inversion (in-VUR-shun)—type of pose in which the head is brought below the heart; standing forward folds, headstands, and handstands are all considered inversions

isometric (eye-suh-MET-rick)—muscle activity in which a tensed position is held steady

modify (MOD-uh-fye)—to change a yoga pose in order to better suit your body

pelvis (PEL-viss)—large bones found at the base of the abdomen

prop (PROP)—a tool used to make different yoga poses easier

Sanskrit (SAN-skrit)—Ancient language from India written from left to right in a script called Devangari

torso (TOR-soh)—the part of the body between the neck and waist, not including the arms

READ MORE

Burns, Brian, Howard Kent, and Claire Hayler. *Yoga for Beginners.* From Couch to Conditioned: A Beginner's Guide to Getting Fit. New York: Rosen Pub., 2011.

Purperhart, Helen. *Yoga Exercises for Teens: Developing a Calmer Mind and a Stronger Body.* Alameda, Calif.: Hunter House Publishers, 2009.

Spilling, Michael, and Liz Lark. *Yoga Step-By-Step.* Skills in Motion. New York: Rosen Central, 2011.

Wood, Alix. *You Can Do Yoga.* Let's Get Moving! Gareth Stevens Publishing: New York, 2014.

INTERNET SITES

FactHound offers a safe, fun way to find Internet sites related to this book. All of the sites on FactHound have been researched by our staff.

Here's all you do:

Visit *www.facthound.com*

Type in this code: 9781491421215

ABOUT THE AUTHOR

Rebecca Rissman is a certified yoga instructor, nonfiction author, and editor. She has written books about history, culture, science, and art. Her book *Shapes in Sports* earned a starred review from *Booklist* magazine, and her series *Animal Spikes and Spines* received *Learning Magazine*'s 2013 Teachers Choice for Children's Books. She lives in Portland, Oregon, with her husband and daughter, and enjoys hiking, yoga, and cooking.

Index